AF425519

Lines About Life

by

Jim McBride

Copyright © 2021
All Rights Reserved
by Jim McBride

Cover design
by Amber Brevard

Printed in the USA

WARNING

No part of this publication may be reproduced, stored in a retrieval system, or transmitted in any form by any means, electronic, mechanical, photocopying, recording or otherwise, without the prior written permission of the author.

Hard back ISBN: 979-8-9854165-0-3
Paper back ISBN: 979-8-9854165-1-0
e-book ISBN: 979-8-9854165-2-7

https://www.facebook.com/jluckyflynn/

https://www.youtube.com/channel/
UCeY4-mEU9Mv4F7rje7NXE7w

Dedicated to

Mom and Dad.

Forever in my heart.

CONTENTS

Lines About Life
By Jim McBride

I was blessed to spend thirty-five years of my life writing songs for a living on world famous Music Row in Nashville, Tennessee, Music City, USA. Songwriting was my job and in great part who I was. During those years, I labored over a guitar until I became a little humpbacked. I always had a pen and legal sized note pads nearby. A pad by the bed, a pad in the living room, a pad in the den and a pad in the hall. Okay, not in the hall. Sadly, during most of those years I burned through about a million cigarettes while writing my songs. I honestly thought I could not write without them. What a dummy!

During the years I lived in Nashville, and wrote professionally for a music publisher, I lost years of sleep, if eight hours a night be the goal for good health. I was either writing a song, thinking about writing a song or dreaming about writing a song. Even as a child, bedtime was a terrible imposition on me. My parents, in order to have a little time to rest without worrying about what I was into, insisted I go to bed at 9:00 p.m. Many nights of my young life were spent wide awake with no one to talk to. Guess I was getting in a little practice for the future.

A boy can get a lot of thinking done at night, if he can whip the Ole Sandman. It seems he gave up on me when I was around six years old. The fear of missing something also played a part in my youthful insomnia. What if something really cool happened during the night and I missed it. Always the last one asleep at home, in the barracks, in a tent, wherever. The sleepless and lonely hours between sunset and sunrise served me well as it turned out. That's when I decided I was gonna do something great someday. I did a lot of night-time daydreaming about inventing something that people would buy just because they thought it was awesome, and had to have one. I had no idea what that invention was.

When I was twelve years old, it hit me. A song. I'll invent a new song, a song never heard before.

From my earliest memory, I loved listening to the radio in our home. The old table model Philco Special, circa 1945, was where I honed my imagination listening to shows like; *The Lone Ranger, Gene Autry, Roy Rogers and Dale Evans, Superman, Sargent Preston of the Royal Canadian Mounted Police, The Green Hornet,* and many more. Of course, we listened to the *Grand Ole Opry,* as well as Big Band Music, and Western Swing, on the only entertainment apparatus in the house. Did I mention we didn't have a television until I was seven years old? I still have that magical, wonderful, memory filled radio.

While, my Mother sang, my Daddy whistled and hummed, and I soaked it all in like a boat bailer sponge. Furthermore, I was enthralled by the tales the old folks told about haints, panthers, accidental exhumations of Cherokee Indian artifacts, bootleggers, hunting trips and kinfolk who were... Uh, shall we say, being provided room and board by the taxpayers for straying beyond the confines of the law, local, state and federal, not to mention the Ten Big Ones in the Bible. Great song material for free. Thanks family!

by Jim McBride

Two huge moments occurred when I was twelve years old. Number one, I took the first paper route money I earned and bought a baby blue GE transistor radio. It was about the size of a Hav-A-Tampa Cigar Box. Hallelujah! I was lonely no more. On the pillow, and next to my ear, that radio was my friend, and it played music for me for hours, until I finally fell asleep. Later, I would purchase another transistor smaller than the first one. It was a Motorola, and it fit in my shirt pocket allowing me to listen to music while on my paper route. Side note: I prayed for cool weather during the World Series each October. If it was cool enough, I could wear a long sleeve shirt, run the earphone wire from the radio inside the pocket of my shirt and down the sleeve. I could prop my head up with my hand covering the earphone, and listen to the Series while pretending to pay attention in class. Creativity, imagination and innovation are gifts from God and we need to use them.

The other milestone, occurring when I was twelve, would later feel like a millstone at times. Remember that song I said I was going to write? Well, I wrote it. It was a song about *Billy the Kid*, the infamous outlaw of the Old West.

Not being able to come up with a melody of my own, in truth, I only invented the lyrics to the song. Fortuitously, a song about Davy Crockett had been a big hit a couple of years earlier and I liked it a lot. It had a very catchy melody so I "borrowed" it from George Bruns who wrote it. Next, I threw out the original lyrics, written by Thomas Blackburn, about Ole Davy, and wrote some new ones.

In doing so, I learned my first lesson in songwriting. I learned about metering. Metering is the way the lyrics lay upon the melody. Billy the Kid was not in sync with the music. It sounded awkward and hurt my ears when I sang it. However, the writing muse said to me, "Try using Billy the Kid's pseudonym". Voilà! "William, William Bonny", fit just like, "Davy, Davy Crockett" over the melody. Another lesson learned. If the line you are using doesn't work, find one that does. My "invention" was of course never recorded or on the radio, so there was no reason for Mr. Bruns to sue a twelve-year-old kid in Alabama who had no knowledge of copyrights and such. If imitation is the sincerest form of flattery, then I flattered him real good. In any case, I was hooked from that day forward. Although, it would be several years before I learned to play guitar, and write my own melodies, and several more years before I made the move to Nashville to be a professional songwriter.

Writing songs in Nashville had been a long-time dream of mine. No one in my family had ever done anything like that. Most of them were wonderful, decent, hardworking, righteous people, except for the aforementioned members of the Alabama prison chain gangs. I guess I just had bigger dreams. I wanted to see the world and do exciting things most of my family didn't even think about. I respected that, and God bless them.

Looking back, it took a while to realize what I was supposed to be doing for a living. For fourteen years, before I was a songwriter, I was a mailman, later known as a letter carrier. It was a great job for a guy who only had a high school education, but there were drawbacks. First of all, the

old saying about the weather and the mail and appointed rounds is for real. It's especially real in the dead of winter and the dog days of summer. Speaking of dogs, I probably have more mail route dog stories than I do songs. Like people, there are good dogs, and there are bad dogs. There are large, scary, over protective dogs who will eat you alive on Saturdays when the kids are in the yard. Beware! Mean dogs don't care what you call yourself, they just hate you for coming by their house in a uniform. Years later, the legendary singer/songwriter John Prine and I, sat in Brown's Diner and traded bad dog stories for two hours. Having been a mailman himself in earlier years, he had his share of canine tales.

However, worse than dogs and foul weather, was having to report to the post office at the ridiculous hour of six a.m. I already told you I was a seasoned non-sleeper. Another imposition on me, courtesy of the city school system, was the asinine hour some sadist chose for the morning bell to ring. I was just getting settled in when it was time to arise and go to school, where I ofttimes finished my nap in class. Same thing with the Army. No, even worse. The day started at 5:30 a.m., and I didn't like it at all. I have found most of my songwriter friends are as nocturnal as I have always been. I think it comes with the territory. There's a reason you hear more songs about sunsets than sunrises.

At long last, in my thirty-third year, I arrived on Music Row with a sack full of songs and a publishing deal that paid me a little over half of what I had been earning as a mailman. It was the best pay cut ever. Now, my job was to write songs all day and leave the nine to five world behind. It was finally nice to say I was a professional songwriter instead of a mailman who wrote songs. This did not preclude some folks asking the question all songwriters hate. "So, what's your real job?" My publishing deal was guaranteed for one year at the previously mentioned pay cut salary, which was actually an advance on future royalties. If you look up the food chain, you will find songwriters furiously trying to get off the bottom. I had a wife and two kids to support, and a one-year guarantee with no benefits, instead of a government job with great benefits. No pressure there. Luckily, I had a taste of success before the move and I was too excited to be scared. Thanks, Jerry Foster and Bill Rice, for giving me the chance to live my dream. Anybody want to record a song written by the new kid in town?

I could not believe how blessed I was to be working with, and becoming friends with, many of my musical heroes. For many years, I had listened to songs written by these awesome songwriters. Their names were in small print beneath the song titles on the 45 records I bought and played. I knew the songs they had written, and where the writers were from, and any other information about them I could find. Now, I could hardly believe I was one of them, not on their level, but working at the same publishing company. I started to have some hits and I began to believe I belonged in this Disneyland of Music. The inhabitants there were so creative, talented, witty and big hearted. I was happy to be welcomed in.

As I began to get my songs recorded, I was over the moon to see my songs and my name on albums sandwiched in between some of my heroes like Harlan Howard, Bill Anderson and Max D. Barnes, all Nashville Songwriter Hall of Fame members.

My first mentor was another Hall of Fame member, Curly Putman. I was thrilled to be on a Keith Whitley album along with Curly. I felt like it justified his belief in me, even before I made the move to Nashville. His encouragement was priceless. Thanks Curly.

The conversations I had with my heroes, over the years planted the idea for all that is to come on the following pages of this book. You see, in my conversations with them, they rarely spoke of the world-wide hit songs they had written. They spoke instead of songs they loved and believed in, but were never able to get recorded. They wanted to share the messages in those songs with the people who loved other songs they had written. It happened over and over again. They would speak of songs recorded by a huge artist like George Jones or Eddie Arnold, recorded, but never released for a myriad of reasons. No matter the reason, the disappointment and heartbreak involved was, and is, not for the weak of spirit. All successful songwriters can tell you stories about the hits that never happened. As the years went by, I began to realize that someday I would be on the other side of that conversation, talking about songs I believed in, but could never bring out into the sunshine to share with the people.

I have been so blessed in my life, I decided to share the most meaningful parts of a few songs you may have heard, and many others from songs you will probably never hear. Words written from years of experience and observation. Thoughts written by my own hand, or co-written with others. Others, who live, dream and die by that glorious, bittersweet, double edged sword called songwriting. These are not poems, but rather, lyrics wrought from emotions we all share.

 I hope you get a blessing from
Lines About Life.
Jim

"Here's to those forevers

That will never come to pass

Sweet words in verses written

Of a love not meant to last

And here's to dreams that die

Or just get lost along the way

Broken hearts and songs

That never see the light of day"

Tommy Conners / Jim McBride

Lines About Life

Youth

I was raised in the shadow of an old cotton mill
Back when believin' was the style
Small town Heaven and a big-eyed boy
Made sweet music for awhile

Weeds and flowers start the same
They all need sun and they all need rain

I was born in a hurry with my hand on the throttle
Momma and daddy's first make and model

We knew Jesus was the answer and Elvis was the king
"Blue Suede Shoes" and "Rock of Ages"
Were the songs we learned to sing
Innocence went out of style and we just watched it go

We worked all day and ran all night
We were hell on wheels with our lights on bright

We were young and fun with nerves of steel
Crazy as a three-ring circus on wheels

Got my real education from the tv station
And good ole boys down at the park

Lines About Life 

I remember the old folks sittin' 'round talkin'
On laid back Sunday afternoons
They said them young folk sure got a hard road
Ah, they're growin' up too soon

When you're young
Everything's crucial
You don't wait around
For parental approval

Me and GI Joe and Jolly Roger
On a raft of cypress logs and twine
Gonna sail to Mobile Bay together
Momma said be home by suppertime

I reckin' I was born
With a restless soul
Standing on a keg of dynamite
There's fire in the hole

Some guys wake up early
Some guys wake up late
Either way, a boy grows up
And a man takes his place

Down by the river on a Friday night

A pyramid of cans in the pale moonlight

Talkin' 'bout cars

And dreamin' 'bout women

Never had a plan

Just alivin' for the minute

When you come from a family

Where thorns and thistles run deep

The fruit you bear is bittersweet

Well, I'm livin' way too fast

I don't know how long I'll last

Hangin' out and stayin' up

May do me in

Summertime came to Sycamore Street

They were seventeen and crazy from the heat

Pull back the curtain

No time to rehearse

Ain't life the

Greatest show on earth

So, take my ticket, tear it in half

I want a front row seat and

A back stage pass

I'll hold my breath, close my eyes
Let fate take me for a ride

Page | 14

My pockets full of hard-earned money
Gonna drive away in a dream
I walked onto that used car lot
Eighteen and green as could be

Living life in the left-hand lane
Just can't wait to go insane
No time to piddle, no time to whittle
There's always a little bit of ground to gain
Living life in the left-hand lane

DREAMS

If every dream we dreamed came true

Wouldn't dreaming lose its value

Life is like an ocean

And I hear it calling me

To trade the safety of the harbor

For the mystery of the sea

We had a dream

But it melted away

Like a box of Crayola

On a hot summer day

I don't know why I stay on

Year after year

It's been a long time since I've dreamed

That dream that brought me here

You gotta dream beyond your doubt

To learn what life is all about

No alibis, just your best try

Lines About Life 

When I sail let me sail in deep waters
Till I can't see dry land anymore
Till the wind will carry me no farther
Lord, if I'm gonna drown
Don't let it be
Too close to the shore

For a while we lived a fantasy
Far away from reality
Oh, how I hated waking from that dream

Did you know I've loved you all my life
It was love long before it was love at first sight
I had the dream long before it came true
There was always the promise of you

What kind of crazy
Would shoot for the moon
Rollin' the dice
Like there's nothing to lose

Hard Times

You know times are tough
When the wolf is at the door
Just beggin' to come in
And sleep there on the floor

My daddy worked hard
Down at the factory
Nights he went to GI School
Didn't know nothin' 'bout a silver spoon
But he lived by the golden rule

I had a plan that seemed foolproof
But it found a crack and
Fell right through

Could be tomorrow
There will come up a wind
To blow all this bad news away

Down on your luck is no disgrace
But pride is expensive, so is saving face

Lines About Life 

Yeah, times are hard
But the good Lord knows
Things could be worse
My name ain't Job

You could tell he was down
By the stoop in his shoulders
And the shine on the seat of his jeans

If you've ever been there
You know how it feels
To watch life go flying by
While you're just spinning your wheels

It's a hard town to live in
It's a hard town to leave

It was paper plates and Dixie Cups
An old Chevrolet that ran on luck

That big diamond ring
Is still just a dream
But I've never heard you complain

Your IRA is in the ICU
They sent your job to Timbuktu
You got forty-three dollars in a Mason Jar
Buried by the swing out in the back yard

Bills you can't pay
Put a strain on devotion

I worry 'bout things I can't seem to change
And wonder what I'm doin' wrong

I've got too much gray for a man of my age
And I'm hooked on these ole cigarettes
I've worked hard all my life and sometimes I wonder
If this is as good as it gets

We may never build that house on the hill
Maybe it's not meant to be

These are the new hard times
Seems like a dollar ain't worth a dime
And we all got caught at the scene of the crime

We can't rob Peter
And we can't pay Paul
To heck with the bankers
God help us all

I was born in a tired old town

With coal dust on my heels

We worked the mines and factories

Till our souls were black and blue

And went to sleep under

A hard luck moon

Love

What if I loved you for a lifetime
Would your heart mind
A little sunshine

I'm slidin' on a rainbow
Swingin' on a star
Sailin' on a sea of love
Every time I'm in your arms

I'm foolin' with the feelin' of fallin' in love

Ain't it strange the way your heart
Can change your mind
Make you see that love ain't love
Unless it's blind

My heart would break if you should leave
'Cause it still feels
Like love to me

Nothing's changed where I'm concerned
That same fire for you still burns

I never believed in what I couldn't see
But you've shown me that feelings
Are all that you need

Lines About Life

I'm looking at love

From a new point of view

Now that I've had it with you

If you only knew

How long I've wanted to

Feel it like I dreamed it

When I was dreaming about you

Oh, the fire of love

Draws you in and burns you up

We can wish on forever but

Darlin' just in case

Let's live for the moment and

Love for today

When troubles come like ocean waves

Weaker hearts might be afraid

But there's no fear for I have you

And there's no storm we can't sail through

Don't think about the past

Don't count the cost

Time here is all you spent

Love's all you lost

I've been in the heat of battle
Where just a few survived
The thought of holding you again
Helped me make it back alive

You can't find love in a bottle
Love's a different kind of strong

I know it's no excuse
But, I thought it was the truth
I love you was just an honest lie

When the storm clouds gather and the rains pour down
When the river of life rages all around
Darlin' don't you worry, don't you be afraid
I won't let it wash you away

Let's take the world out of this
Till what we have is all there is

Ain't it strange how love can take
A heart that's hard as steel
Hold it tightly in the fire
And teach that cold heart how to feel

Who would have thought for any reason
Winter would turn out to be
The sweetest season of them all
Like a late-night fire, like a hand in a glove
Our hearts are warm
In our November love

I try and try to reach you
But I can't read your mind
You know you make it hard
To love you sometimes

I need you when the winds of winter
Bring long nights of sweet desire
To feel you hold me close and
Slowly build a raging fire

When you love someone
You always put them first
You learn how to forgive
Even when it hurts

Love and lust defy rational thinkin'

Who fired first don't matter now
We turned this house into a battleground

You know love don't need a lawyer
Love's not guilty of a crime

It was a storm without the thunder
It was a death without a grave
Like a ship going under
Quietly love slipped away

I know I should know better
Love sure took me to school
The best thing I have ever felt
Left me feeling like a fool

I don't remember anything you said
That might have hurt me
So, what on earth would make you
Think you don't deserve me
I only heard three words
Come out of your mouth
Anything you said before
I love you don't count

You can bet your heart on me
Honey, you can be a winner

 Lines About Life

Love is the hardest lesson I've ever learned

The sun going down takes my breath away
What a beautiful end to a near perfect day
The best part of all is I spent it with you
I'm the luckiest man this side of the moon

What would you do if I told you
I want you night and day
If I told you you're always on my mind
What would you say

What if our worlds could be just one
What if that dream came true
What if I said
I love you

I think it's fair to say
I have never loved this way

There's a razor-sharp thin line
Between love and hate sometimes

It was hard to tell
Who loved who more
But that was back
Before the war

When I'm holding you, I lose all sense of time
It's the only time forever, ever comes to mind

I love you to the edge and back
It's like a high wire act
Like bein' blindfolded
With a hard wind blowin'
And knowin' there's no net

Forever's too far
For hearts that are blind
Love will get lost
When it's left behind

That old lonely road I've been on
Has finally reached the end and
This is where forever begins

Too beautiful for words
That's what you are
Even new to the day
You shine like a star

It would only take forever
To ever thank you for your smile
But to let you know how much I love you
Now, that might take awhile

You're the music and the words
To the sweetest song I've ever heard

Took an ad out in the paper
Sold my old Corvette
Been moonlightin' at McDonald's
Just to clear up all my debts
I'll do anything that's legal
Just to buy that diamond ring
Don't that prove I love you
More than anything

Love is more than just a game
That's why it hurts so much to lose it

Where does love go when it's lost
There's no marble stone
No wooden cross

Love me like I'm leavin'
Like I'm never coming back
It's been such a long time
Since you loved me like that

When I feel your final touch
And I give my last breath up
I'll leave knowing I was loved
Because of you

Can't stop the leaves from fallin'
Or that whippoorwill callin'
Can't stop the sky from turnin' blue
Can't stop the sun from shinin'
Or the moon from risin'
Can't stop thinkin' about you

I've always been just a face in the crowd
Just a run of the mill kind of guy
But why should I care what the world thinks of me
You think I'm one of a kind

Out on the horizon where the earth meets the sky
That old man is rising to light up the night
You reach for my hand and I'm touched by the truth
I'm the luckiest man this side of the moon

I can't keep this love alive
I can't save it by myself
So, it's gonna be goodbye
If you don't give me some help

I know what it's like to love till it hurts
It's thunder on lightnin' and Heaven on earth

We're so close I can't tell
Where you end and where I start
If I loved you anymore
I would need another heart

I wish I could touch you
Till you know how much you
Keep makin' me feel like a man
But I've only got two hands

I'm always amazed you remember the day
The hour, the minute, the moment we met
I can't even recall if it was springtime or fall
But that feeling is one thing I'll never forget

You're a different kind of sweet
Strong and totally unique
The kind that God knew I would need
To tie me down and set me free

It might be right off the top of my head
But it's coming from the bottom of my heart

Life just keeps getting better each day
Feels like everyday is Friday at five
And I just got paid

There's a thread that runs
Through the sands of time
Like a mighty rollin' river
It's the heart and soul
Of the ties that bind
It's the gift that gives to the giver

If I had to choose
What to keep and what to lose
It wouldn't be hard to do
'Cause all I need is you

We call it the scene of the crime
Where we met for the very first time
We still talk of how loneliness died
That night at the scene of the crime

How long will I love you
I don't really know
I'd like to think forever
Is how far we could go

Lines About Life 

I'm learning to love rainy days
I feel good even when skies are gray
Since you've been around
They don't get me down
I'm learning to love rainy days

Moonlight on a summer night
Does strange things to the heart

Love's got a good side
A bad side too
It's good when you've got it
And bad when it's through

I like fallin' in love, I'll admit it
It's a habit I picked up a long time ago

If you can recall
When we had it all
Your memory is better than mine

I don't fly in bad weather
And I don't set sail
When the seas are rough
So, why am I unafraid
To put my heart in harm's way
Every time I fall in love

Bad things happen to us all
Troubles pin us to the wall
When I see those dark clouds comin'
I start looking for my woman

Nobody falls in love
Not wanting to stay
Only a fool would
Do it that way

They say the new wears off
Just give it time
But the older our love gets
The more it seems to shine

Bought the best of Barry Manilow
'Cause you love to hear him sing
Don't that prove I love you
More than anything

If we never look for
That love we once lived for
We will never find it again
And we'll lose our one chance to win

I'm up against a memory
The one you won't let go
It's always there between us
When I try to hold you close

Love don't rhyme with politics, dirty tricks or get rich quick
Love don't rhyme with education, occupation or who you know

Same old song we've heard before
'Bout broken hearts and slamming doors
Just never dreamed it would be us
But then again
Who does

Don't we all promise
To love, honor and trust
But time alone proves
Who don't and who does

You don't need to worry
About what comes to pass
This old world may wear out
But my love's gonna last

by Jim McBride

TEMPTATION

Now, some can face temptation
Turn around and walk away
But I'm the kind who'll stand in line
For just one little taste

I'm not saying he's a liar
He's just got a way with words
He can paint a picture
Like none you've ever heard
So be careful when you're listening to
A story telling man

When the Devil made addiction
He made it sweet and strong
Make a man lose his convictions
His family and everything he owns

I know Satan has his demons
On his left and on his right
But I'm bringing Jesus with me
To the fight

The Devil lives in Hollywood
And vacations in Las Vegas

I never was this sober on Saturday night
I used to swim that whiskey river side to side

I was standing at the crossroads
Frozen in my tracks
Afraid to take the next step
The one you can't take back

I look in the mirror
And see another man's face
I really don't know where I've gone
And who has taken my place

You're worse than a bar that opens at ten
With two-dollar beer and ESPN

My heart keeps changin' sides
In this fight between wrong and right

She's never been to the Wayside Inn
She's never been this far down the road to sin
She'll never be the same again
After she checks out of the Wayside Inn

She was hotter than a two-dollar pistol
In a paper sack
Tore off with my heart
In the trunk of her Cadillac

You could say that he was in
A perilous position
Diggin' a hole straight to Hell
Like a man on a mission

Late one-night last summer
While he was up in Charlotte
For a little while a good man
Put his conscience in his pocket

I was headed for Hell
With one hand on the wheel
And one on a bottle of wine

Now, you know the dog that bit you
Is in a bottle behind the bar
Might as well go for the bottom
You've already come this far

 Lines About Life

He's the star of all his stories
The cowboy, captain and the king
Before you even know it
You'll believe most anything

Once, his passion burned so bright
Surely there must be an ember
Somewhere deeper
Than that whiskey river flows

I swear I don't know
Which demon came first
A lonely man's hunger
Or a crazy man's thirst

My TV says there ain't no sin
Anything goes
So, I bought in

He was still a young man
When he gave in to the bottle
And that first swallow
Washed his pride away

It scares me to think

How much time I've spent

With two strikes against me

Three sheets to the wind

The Devil lives across the county line

Preacher said that a thousand times

Yeah, he's just waitin' on down the road

To snatch you up and steal your soul

Like sixty-one and forty-nine

There's lots of crossroads in this life

Decisions that you have to make

Which highway you gonna take

Every time I give the Devil a ride

He wants to drive

by Jim McBride

HURT

There's a hurt even Shakespeare
Couldn't put into words

Love hurts bad
When it's unrequited
But you can't go
Where you're not invited

How did the good times
Get lost in the hurt
What made us think
It couldn't get any worse
If this ain't the bottom
Lord, I don't know what is
'Cause even the bad times
Were better than this

Our great expectations
Of how love should be
Broke apart on the hard rocks
Of reality

Lines About Life

Time won't heal the pain until
Your heart has hurt enough
But, there's an anchor always there
For those who trust in love
Hearts that don't give up

If I could point my finger
Put all the blame on you
Then maybe I'd feel better
'Bout this pain I'm goin' through
But if these walls could talk
They would lay the blame right at my feet

If I had found the strength
To make my move a little sooner
I might have saved my heart a scar or two

She was painfully honest
I was hopelessly hurt
To know the truth or not to know
I wonder which is worse

He was bound for glory
And she was bound to be
Just another footnote
In his biography

Everybody tried to tell me
She would break my heart in two
But I told everybody
You don't know her like I do

Something is wrong when you're
The only one who sacrifices
The only one who ever stops
To wonder what the price is

Maybe your heart needed breakin'
Maybe some tears had to fall
Just to let you know you can take it
And you will survive after all

You don't know how hard it is
Just breathing in and out like this

The sooner I start hurtin'
The sooner I'll be done

I'll give it to you truthful
Truthful, pure and plain
I don't drink whiskey for the pleasure
I drink it for the pain

Maybe someday I'll be alright

Maybe someday

But not tonight

I'm not doing well

I don't like the story

Time had to tell

I never got better

I only got worse

You can't do nothin'

With this kind of hurt

Either you're the world's worst cheater

Or you don't really care

Dishonesty is one thing honey

But you ain't cheatin' fair

It's all I can do to look at you

And not give in

Wish you hadn't made forgivin'

You so hard

On my heart

But you did

by Jim McBride

I hurt 'cause I drink

I drink 'cause I hurt

I go back and forth

Between bad and worse

I could see it comin' from a mile away

A heartache lookin' for a place to stay

Tomorrow the storm clouds may roll over me

But everywhere you go it's gonna rain

The sun still comes up

The world still goes 'round

Don't ask me why, I don't know

I've done all I can do

To turn yesterday loose

But time only tightens the hold

I could see forever

When I was in the dark

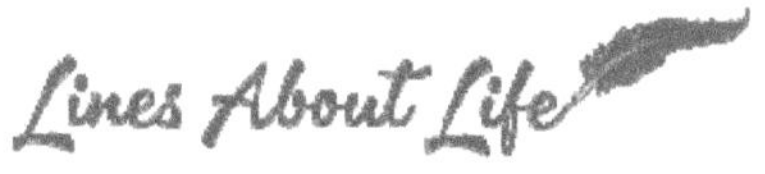Lines About Life

The weeds have overgrown the sandbox
Where he used to play
And it's all she can do
To make it through on his birthday
Life goes on but the laughter's gone
Only memories remain
To follow her from room to room
In this house of pain

I wish I could help you
But my heart tells me not to
It still ain't found the trust
You threw away
So, you can't have it back no matter
How bad you want it, hurts don't it

If only time will heal the hurt
This may last forever
I may never know how it feels
To forget

I guess I must be some kind of fool
Otherwise, I don't know why on earth I'd hurt you

I've got everything a broken heart needs
Oh, I'm doin' fine
Don't you worry 'bout me

Tender hearts are always open
Easily broken and hard to mend

It's a cold day in Heaven tonight
Trust and love are covered up
In a solid sheet of ice
Yeah, we've got trouble here in paradise
It's a cold day in Heaven tonight

I've been steamrolled, bullet-holed and hurricaned

She's only gone when I'm sober
So, I don't stay that way too much these days
When I'm out of my mind, it's not over
She's only gone when I'm sober

I still think of you
Until the morning comes
Then I see your face
In every rising sun
Who was the fool who said
It gets better with time
You're still the perfect picture
To fit my frame of mind

Lines About Life

Sometimes I'm afraid tomorrow won't come

Sometimes I'm afraid that it will

She hurt him like a hard country song

You know a sad one where someone

Got really done wrong

Where the whiskey's too weak

'Cause the memory's too strong

Lord, she hurt him like a hard country song

It's not that hard to do

When you've got two fools

Who don't know what they've got to lose

That's how you break a heart

I could have run for cover

If I'd seen that dark cloud coming

But when you've got no place to go

What's the point in running

Took that trip to love just to feel the pain

Had to walk back home in the pouring rain

If I ever go back I'm gonna take it slow

No use runnin' down a dead-end road

It sure looked good on paper
Love never had a more perfect design
But when hearts go blind
And old feelings die
It's just so many words on a line

I guess what hurts the most is
When you say you can't recall
Even one good memory
From when we had it all

I can't say he's better lookin'
We both know that's a lie
God knows he's not funny
Though Heaven knows he tries
But, there's one thing about him
That just can't be denied
He may not make me laugh that much
But, he never makes me cry

If time really heals like they say it will do
It must only work if your heart wants it to
But the truth never changes
And the past never dies
When you've got a memory like mine

Who were we to think
No one had ever loved like us
Never dreaming for a moment
Love could ever hurt this much

A hangover and a heartache
Make a perfect pair
One keeps me feelin' low down
When the other ain't there

Did you know a full roll of quarters
Will last you 'bout two hours long
And you can get a lot of cryin' done
If you don't play nothin' but sad songs

He's a hopeless situation
Blown by a bitter wind

How can a heartache live forever
Just get older and still stay young

He's a loser's kind of loser
Still lookin' for a friend
In a world that's made for nine by twelve
He's just eight by ten

GOODBYES

Don't make me have to hurt you
I don't want to see you cry
In your heart you know the truth
We've done all that we can do
To keep this love alive

Now I'm on my hands and knees, me and Mister Clean
We're wipin' up your footprints off the floor
I won't leave one single trace
That you were ever in this place

You should be a movie star
Your sad act comes so easy
So, take a bow and don't look back
When you finally leave me

It's too late to say I'm sorry
But it's too soon to say goodbye

Please, don't make this any harder than it is
Let's just say goodbye without a goodbye kiss

She took a long time leavin'
But when she did
That was that
She took a long time leavin'
'Cause she knew
She wasn't coming back

I can tell you're not feelin'
That old feelin' anymore
You've got one eye on the highway
And one foot out the door

There's a great big world of difference
Between who I am
And what you need

Don't let your conscience keep you here
I can make it on my own
There's nothing in this house
You can't live without
So, you might as well be gone

Did you know that one goodbye
Can forever change your life
Haunt you till the day you die

I'm not gonna say it again
I'm just gonna write it on the wall
Maybe it will finally sink in
These two little words that say it all
No more

Go on and walk away
Do what you want
Some hearts take leavin' hard
And some hearts don't

I ain't leavin' Texas baby
I'm just leavin' you

Yesterday meant something,
At least it did to me
But I guess our past is just a ghost
That only I can see

I may fly like an eagle
Or sink like a stone
Laugh when you leave me
Or cry when you're gone

Lines About Life

I've got this funny feelin'
I can't put my finger on it
But it sure feels like we've been here
Before now honey don't it
Did we say we were through
Or is this just a case of Deja blue

The sun shines through her windshield
As she drives away
It's a brand-new tomorrow
Beginning today

If I could have you
I know what I'd do
This time I'd be true
If I had you

I'll stay right here forever
I'll never take one step
I'll hang on till your love is gone
Until there's nothing left

Some people leave and don't come back
Can't turn around on a one-way track

The good Lord knows I dread it
After all that we've been through
To give up on forever
Ain't no easy thing to do

You told me to forget about forever
That you'd be coming back
The day after never

What happened to the passion
We once held in our hands
It came in like a lion
And went out like a lamb

You packed up your life, cried at the door
From that moment on you've been free
Girl, I'm happy for you but
To tell you the truth
It ain't been that easy for me

If your mind's set on leavin'
If that's how it is
Just end it now, don't drag it out
Let's get it over with

Where did the summer go
Who stole the red from off the roses
Growing in the garden
Where we kissed for the first time

Ain't it strange how the darkness
Opens up your eyes
Now I can see where things went wrong
And why she said goodbye

I know what she said
But that ain't how I heard it
A goodbye's still a goodbye
No matter how you word it

If there's no turning back
We can't go on like this
I never did like long goodbyes
Let's get it over with

The last goodbye's the hardest one to take
When the words I'm sorry come too late

There ain't no time like tomorrow
There ain't no place like gone
There's always a river too wide to cross
When you don't really want to go home

by Jim McBride

You lie here in this bed each night

With your back to me

And silence lies between us

Underneath these cold white sheets

Goodbye and whiskey just don't mix

One makes me sad and one makes me sick

Hello Mister Lonesome

Do you hear that whistle blow

You can't stop that goodbye train

Once it starts to roll

Your suitcase is packed

You're leavin' alone

Now you're just a goodbye from gone

I don't want to be your angel anymore

If being good to you is all that I'm good for

You weren't there to see her leave

I guess the clouds got in between

When you see her now

Does she mention me

Old sentimental moon

Lines About Life

She didn't leave, she didn't leave
She didn't leave
She just never came back

How far down this goodbye road
Can I go till I'm too far gone

What about that woman, a victim of a vow
At the mercy of an angry man
And the holier than thou
He says Jesus may have saved you once but
Where's your Jesus now, tell me
How long do you think she ought to stay

I was busy being true to you
On the day your heart left home

It was all that she left him
The night that she left him
So, he clung to her memory with all of his might

Till you do what you should have done

A long, long time ago

Till you can look him in the eye

And say that final goodbye

Gone is only the direction

That you're leanin'

That ain't leavin'

I'm gonna buy me a new pair of shoes

Lace 'em up tight and walk out on you

I'm goin' downtown 'fore this day is through

And I'm gonna buy me a new pair of shoes

Gone like empty, gone like broke

Straight outta here in a puff of smoke

Just light me up dear Lord

And get me gone

I can't stand the thought of leaving

But if staying would be worse

And if it's really over, you go first

You wrestle with the lie you live

Your conscience and your fears

All the while just dyin'

To be anywhere but here

Why don't we just leave
All this leavin' talk aside
Let's not let our hearts become
The victims of our pride

When it's over, it's over
Ain't that the way it's supposed to be
When it's over, it's really over
But right now it's hard to believe
It's ever gonna be over for me

We built this house with love and our own hands
I thought we put forever in the plans
But love's not bound by windows, walls and floors
And all that matters now is just the door

by Jim McBride 

LONELINESS

Lonely is as lonely does

When it's too tough
To tough it out
You hate to see the sun go down

I'm so good at forgettin'
I can't remember me
Brother can you tell me
Who I used to be

It's an all-night thing
Oh, the pain that lonely brings

I've got a lot to learn about leavin'
I've never been where the nights are this long

My heart's like a room
Where the sun never shines

Freedom is a prison to a fool

This ain't where I belong
This ain't no place like home
It's a good thing that leavin's allowed

 Lines About Life

If I could change my memory
If I could lock the truth outside
Then lonely couldn't touch me
And I'd still have my pride

As I sit here by the window in my lonely room
It's two a.m. and no one's on the street
The cold wind blows a cloud across that ole blue moon
Ain't there anybody in this world but me

The morning sun will wash away the night
And I'll see things in a different light
But right now there's no peace of mind for me
'Cause I can't make your memory go to sleep

At a table for two, just me without you
I sit and I think about us

Living like there's no tomorrow
Finally got to me tonight

There's not one piece of sacred ground
In this God forsaken town

I've come a long way

From where you left me

I've spent some long nights here alone

But that's all behind me

Now that I've finally

Got the hang of holdin' on

I was better off believin'

She was all she seemed to be

Even now I know she never

Meant to make a fool of me

As I lie here in the middle of

Another lonely night

Sometimes I wish I'd never

Seen the light

This new place won't feel like home

I'll be here but you'll be gone

I'll never waste money on therapy

Ain't nothin' those doctors can say to me

My head can't help what my heart won't do

And I'll never get used to life without you

I can go where I want
All by myself
I can stay too long
Till I'm the last fool left

Strung out feelin' lonely
Like I've never had a home
Like an orphan walking wide eyed
Down a long dark road
Waking up in cheap motels
Sick of all the sights and smells
Nightmares look a lot like dreams
When you're only seventeen

Broken hearts don't go by the seasons
And loneliness comes and goes as it pleases

Ain't this world a lonely town
When the blues have got you down

Rain, rain don't go away
I'm not ready for a sunny day

Each morning I wake up

In a world I thought I wanted

And wish that it was only a bad dream

From a distance

This pasture sure looked

A whole lot greener

But things ain't always what they seem

You don't have to tell me how it feels

There ain't nothin' about lonesome I don't know

The sound lingers on

And it don't seem that long

Since I used to sing

And you were my song

I'm a man about down

Out on the town

It ain't much of a life

But it's something

It's a new world I've found

But I keep losing ground

I'm a man about down

To nothin'

Lines About Life

I'll be blue enough for two

I've got a fortune in cheap souvenirs
Reminders of memories we made
When you were here
Sometimes they bring laughter
Sometimes they bring tears
You left a fortune in cheap souvenirs

I hid my heart in a deep dark place
Where it could not get away
Couldn't be broken, couldn't be told a lie
Safe and secure from the sound of goodbye

I've got everything a broken heart needs
Oh, I'm doin' fine, don't you worry 'bout me

Old memories stand guard
Like silent wardens in the doorway

It was almost worth it for the time we spent
But there ain't no future in a heart for rent

by Jim McBride

The streets are almost empty
The bars are all closed
The cops have gone for coffee
And the hookers have gone home
They're talkin' 'bout religion
On the radio
I roll down my window
And light another smoke
Where can you go when you can't go home

You're out in California
Not thinkin' about me
You don't care what happens
In the state of Tennessee
But wanting you and weather
Are two things I can't control
So, I'll be thinkin' 'bout you
When that ole blue thunder rolls

Day after tomorrow
You won't be alone
I'll make it all better
The minute I'm home
Just forty-eight hours
Till I'm holding you tight
But, day after tomorrow
Feels like forever tonight

Lines About Life

Sometimes late at night
She thinks she hears him calling
It wakes her up like thunder
And makes her cry like rain

How much is your pride worth
How much would you pay
To get back what it's cost
To keep loneliness away

For a man who was king of the mountain
This old barstool ain't much of a throne
And it's hard waking up to a new day
Knowing all of the good ones are gone

All my friends say I was wrong
That I deserve to be alone
They don't waste their sympathy
On the fool that I turned out to be

Now it's back to the blacktop and the blues
Goin' back to doin' what I do
Back to bein' gone and missin' you
Back to the blacktop and the blues

I've had my share of black coffee
In rooms that you rent by the week
Been stung by the silence of strangers
In towns where misfortune led me

Here I am on honky-tonk highway
It's the loneliest road I've ever been down
There's no hope on this honky-tonk highway
When you can't find a place to turn around

I'm so lonesome I can't cry
There ain't no relief in sight
Love has left me high and dry
The well is out of water

He can't think of one good reason
Why she'd ever want to leave him
Never crossed his mind she'd say goodbye
Now she's gone and he don't get it
It still hasn't hit him yet
It might be how he treated her
And how he made her cry

A silver spoon can't always feed the hunger
Even if you have a heart of gold
Everything you own adds up to nothin'
When you don't have someone you can hold

A sad two-week tour, one last trip back
Revisiting feelings that live in the past
I chased old memories all over creation
That's how I spent my summer vacation

I'm so tired of waking
With my heart still breaking
All for the sake of
This thing we call love

It's cruel, it's cold, it's crazy I know
To stay in a place where you can't even sleep
For the roar of the silence
And the loneliness that never lets up
It's unmerciful
Unmerciful

I've been dreadin' sundown all day long

I know I should be thankful
And I'm trying hard to be
But all the things I didn't do
Eat away at me

I guess I could go crazy
From wondering where you are
But you know, I kinda hate
To go that far

I'm in a tropical depression
I've got the blue water blues

I haven't had a good night's sleep
In weeks now thanks to you
The ghost of broken promises you made
Haunts every room

It's not the dark
It's not a blue northern wind
And it's not the quiet
That's crawlin' all over my skin

Sometimes I wonder why we can't change
Live life like most people do
Stop all this runnin' that keeps us apart
And cure all these telephone blues

There's a flashing neon tombstone
Where a fallen angel fell
Out on heartbreak highway
Got the blues in a bad motel

Lines About Life

by Jim McBride

REGRET

Did you know that pure regret

Can tear a man's heart from his chest

If it was so right, what went wrong

How did it just slip away

If we never look for

The love once we once lived for

We may never find it again

And we lost our one chance to win

If I had a dollar

For every dollar I have lost

I'd stop this crazy ride I'm on

And I'd buy my way off

Bitter words are harder than a stone

And you can't get 'em back once they've been thrown

There's no room in my suitcase for regret

So, I'm just gonna leave it by the door

It still hurts a little

But not why you think it does

It's for the time that I wasted

Believing in us

Time creates a distance of its own
That's why you're still there
And I'm still here
It ain't the miles
It's the years

Standin' on the trap door
With my neck in a noose
My eyes tell the story
I ain't got much to lose

I had to look through our old pictures
To see the way we used to smile
Before we left love in the closet
Like it just went out of style

Don't you know that for every mistake
Eventually
There's a price to be paid

No matter where this road may take me
Time will never make me
Lose this hope I have of
Holding you again

Sadness comes to those who wait

When I love you's said too late

I never knew that I needed you so

And now that I've lost you I can't let you go

In some men's eyes I never made it

And so for me they've no concern

Like a road that leads to nowhere

Like a fire that never burned

The juke box had my number

And the blues played on and on

I said get me a cab 'cause

I'm in no shape to drive home

Then I stumbled to the restroom

While the barkeep made the call and I wrote

There ain't no refuge

For a fool there on the wall

If I'd only let you go the day you left

I'd be lookin' back and wonderin'

What the fuss was all about

If I'd only let you go

I'd be over you by now

Lines About Life 

Sometimes it's hard
To make it easy on yourself

Somewhere along the line you'll see the light
Someday you'll feel the way I feel tonight
Lost love will leave a stain time can't wipe clean
You can't just turn it off like some old machine

You said I'd live to regret it
I said I'll die before I do
Now the pain is gonna kill me if I let it
Has it been a lifetime since I walked out on you

Old memories live on dark quiet streets
Where I never go, till I'm caught in the glow
Of a blue Memphis moon
Sad as the tune that's played in my head
Every day since you left

I just said forgive me
If there's any way you can
But if your heart won't let you
I will understand

I'd rather go to sleep
In a cold lonely bed
Than to wake up next to someone
I wish I'd never met

I miss the old you
I miss the old me
I miss the lovers we used to be

If the door to love's still open
Tell me what I need to do
I could move a mountain
Or I could just hold you

It breaks my heart to see you leave
With nothing but regret
Why can't you remember
What I can't forget

There's a world of difference
Between fear and respect
And it's always been the unknown
That scares me half to death

One night on the dance floor
I held you just for a moment in time
I wish we'd danced all night long

Lines About Life

I get this way sometimes
When I've had a little too much wine
When those old memories return
From across that bridge I couldn't burn

It's a story with no happy ending
A mystery without any clues
A promise that's bound to be broken
A wish that will never come true

I'm the master of mistakes
Made some bad ones in my day

I could say you never loved me
But that wouldn't be the truth
'Cause if only for a little while
You were mine to lose

Don't listen when your heart tells you it's over
Or you'll end up with a heartache just like mine
What's it gonna hurt to say you're sorry
'Cause loneliness don't care who's wrong or right

I knew she was crying on her pillow
I rolled over 'cause I couldn't face the truth
Just three inches of silence lay between us
One word could have changed it all
But my lips just wouldn't move

There won't be a wall of hurt so wide
That I can't reach around
There won't be this chain of broken dreams
To hold me down
When I get over you

Some changes are good
Some changes are bad
I got what I wanted
But I lost what I had
Sometimes I'd give anything
To get a few things back

I know I should be thankful Lord
I'm trying hard to be
But all the things I didn't do
Eat away at me

Lines About Life

There's a pay phone at the end of this bar
But my foolish pride won't let me go that far
I'd pay any price it takes to make her mine again
So why am I still starin' at this quarter in my hand

I'd like to wake up early
And wear a smile all day
I'd love to feel the way I felt
Before you went away
But the earth still turns with no concern
For how I feel inside
I want the world the way it was
When you were mine

REDEMPTION

Time is the taker of everything
Only the soul and love remain

We all need to know God's word
Book, chapter and verse

I've been out there
In the great unknown
Now, praise the Lord
I'm goin' home

Every scar tells a story
And the greatest one of all
Was written down in red
With three nails and a cross

I'm over the influence
Clear eyed and sober
Free to be the real me
Now that it's over

What if you were a picture God had never painted
What if you were a poem without words
What if you were a dream
I never dared to dream I deserved
What if you were a song I never heard

Lines About Life

You say you're not a slave to the bottle anymore
You say you finally slipped out
Of the Devil's own back door

Starting today ain't easy to do
After what yesterday put me through

Here you go down the road you took
Write another chapter in your own little book
Forgive yourself for Heaven's sake
Don't pay twice for the same mistake

There's no new way home
You still have to go past
The old rugged cross

Do you feel unworthy
Do you think all hope is lost
Are your hands so dirty
You can't get the guilty off
Well, there's mercy like a river
Flowing from above

Here's what I learned
While I was down on my knees
God has an answer for everything

I've been thinkin' 'bout a new start
Somewhere sane to get my mail
Gonna shake this monkey off my back
And the Devil off my trail

Keep me in your grace
Help me show the world a better face

You can talk to God for free
If you're thinkin' 'bout repentin'
But it's still gonna cost you
'Cause I ain't that forgivin'

I'm finally where I belong
Dancing with you to this song
One I never would have written
If you had not come along

Mistakes, I've made a few
The kind you can't undo
Said I'm sorry till I was blue in the face

Can't you hear the church bells ringin' all over town
Waking saints and sinners alike
The good Lord spends his Sundays trying to win back
What he lost to the Devil on Saturday night

WISDOM

Love builds the bridges
Pride builds the walls

What could be more sad
What could be more wrong
Than a man who's most remembered
For always being gone

How much is enough
What's the point of being richer
If you miss out on the memories
And you're never in the pictures

There's a wisdom that you earn
When your life has come full turn

You gotta believe it's gonna get better
Life will be good one of these days
You gotta be strong
When the world turns on you
And when you dream
You gotta believe

Hands build a house, hearts build a home

I know my days are numbered
How many, time will tell
So, if I want to waste one fishin'
I say, might as well

Just think about life like a ten-dollar bill
To waste or spend wisely whichever you will
Ain't it strange how we don't
Think too much about time
Till we get down to
Pennies, nickels and dimes

Ain't no use lookin' over your shoulder
For a long-lost four-leaf clover

You can turn out the lights
In a house with no curtains
But heartache has nowhere to hide

I guess that's what memories are for
When you can't go back there anymore

Why do I let troubles make me
Look at life like it's a war
One day it won't matter anymore

Now, everyone's life tells a story
But the ending is not always the same
The only difference between Hell and Glory
Is where you're standing when it starts to rain

I don't wear a watch; I know what time it is
If it ain't time for that then it's time for this
I know it's of the essence
And if you hurry up and wait
You can buy yourself a little
But it don't matter anyway
It's all God's time

We can blame it all
On that clock there on the wall
But it's our fault
We let it boss us around

You gotta swing your hammer with a steady stroke
Blow by blow till the big rock's broke

If you live long enough
Then you must face the truth
You can't clip the wings
On the sweet bird of youth

I know I don't know everything
But there's one thing I've discovered
Every prayer gets answered
In one way or another

I've been left out in the cold
I've been tried by fire
Heaven knows the price I've paid
For the wisdom I've acquired

Let the little things be little
Don't let them take up too much room
In that special place where you keep
What means the most to you

There's nothing quite as hopeless
There's nothing quite as sad
As trying to hold on to
What you never really had

If the past ain't pretty
It's too late to paint it
Today is all we've got to work with
Ain't it

Sometimes nothin'
Is better than somethin'
If somethin' brings nothin'
But heartache and doubt

Sooner or later
It all becomes what used to be

Hard right turns may be difficult to make
But they'll always lead you
Down the road that you should take

You never know what tomorrow might bring
But you can't go wrong when you do the right thing

Sometimes it's not the fall that kills you
Sometimes it's the tryin' to get back up

The past has had its say
That's why they call it yesterday

Fame and fortune come and go
Got a high price don't you know

Lines About Life

When you run out of alibis
Can't even find a weak excuse
The only thing left standing is
The truth

Yesterday's only a fool's destination

She lived sixty odd years with the same old man
She's got home grown wisdom and time worn hands

When you're standing at the crossroads
Where deception meets the truth
Listen to your heart
When it tells you what to do

Guilt cuts like a razor
And the truth ain't much on favors
When you try to write it down
On a piece of plain white paper

What gives us the right
To cast the first stone
To be somebody's judge and jury too

Angry words cut quick and deep
It's hard to hide that injury

Some things are just meant to last
And the present's just part of the past

Are you just running out the clock
Can't smell the roses if you don't stop
So, breath it in, take it slow
The world goes on, but you won't...
And I won't

Runnin' with the big dogs might excite you
But sooner or later they're gonna bite you

They say no good deed goes unpunished
But it ain't about pride
And it ain't about money

Can't be too careful of the company you keep
Some people don't know
When they're gettin' in too deep

It's hard to keep your head on straight
When your feet don't touch the ground

Promises are just
Made for those who trust
Unafraid they take forever
For the Gospel truth

There's giving too much
There's staying too long
And there's worse things
Than being alone

We can't count on tomorrow
It's all borrowed time
And there's no guarantee
The sun is gonna shine

Perhaps the good Lord gave men hair
So they'd seek out the barber's chair
A place of refuge for an hour
Where rich and poor have equal power

Now sanity is a state of mind
Where life begins
Or where it ends
It all depends

Got no formal education
But I get gratification
From my simple vocation
I like working with my hands

Here's what's wrong with the world today
The almighty dollar is running the place

Music

I was only nine when I found out what the blues is

Lord, I loved the way they played

They did it for the music

If I wrote a song about that

If I said it in a way

No one ever had

Would it light a spark

Would it bring you back

They use it in the church house

And the honky-tonks

Sometimes salvation

Starts with a song

I'm just one great song away

Baby, that's all it's gonna take

We'll be livin' next door

To Dolly someday

I'll sing for you, but not for long

I'm just one note in time's great song

I don't want to be around
When they bring down the curtain
When you can't sing a real song
About lovin' and hurtin'

I heard your new song today
I don't like the words
But the melody's great
It's an interesting take on the truth
The way it all went down
According to you

Once it's in your blood
There's nothing you can do
Once it gets a hold it won't let go
I was just a kid when music took control
Sent a shiver up my spine
Touched something in my soul

There are all kinds of songs on the jukebox
You can pick one that hits close to home
Which one would you choose if I told you
It's the last time that you'll hear that song

Have you listened to the songs

Of the man from Georgiana

Have you ever been so lonesome

You could cry

If nothin' else had ever

Come from down in Alabama

At least we still could sing

"I Saw the Light"

Have you ever heard the story

Of the deal made at the crossroads

'Tween the Devil and

The "King of Delta Blues"

Mister Johnson took the train

All the way up to Chicago

Just to find the Devil

Always gets his due

Daddy won a radio

Tuned it to a country show

I was rockin' in the cradle

To the cryin' of a steel guitar

He sang "Born to Lose"

He put his heart in it

When he sang that line

About livin' in vain

He really meant it

A sad six string and a jukebox voice

I'm the lonely people's choice

I was made to play the part

I was born with a broken heart

Shovel on some fiddle

Shovel on some banjo

Shovel on some bass

Shovel on some mando

Stoke it with the guitar

Till it starts to smoke

Till we feel it in our soul

We're pourin' on the coal

If she don't ask

Who's that singin'

When you're listening to Merle

Marry that girl

I know the odds are against me

I know it's gonna be tough

But when it comes to rollin' the dice

I've always had good luck

I'm gonna stand up on that Opry stage

With my initials on my boots

And shine like Porter Wagoner's suit

I've lived my life, I've spent my time

Searching for that perfect rhyme

So, I think I'll just close the door

And lock up all these metaphors

I don't think I'll write a song today

FUN

I know we're a little screwed up

Probably need psychiatry

But I'm helping her

And she's helping me

Work on our co-dependency

I don't know my number

Never took an IQ test

I'd say somewhere between

Edison and Einstein

If I had to make a guess

If I keep on goin' crazy

I'll get there by and by

Since you've been gone

I sit by the phone

Feelin' like the Maytag Man

Crazy is a lot more fun

Yeah, crazy is a lot more fun

Let the people talk about the things I've done

Crazy is a lot more fun

If you were the only man in the world

I'd just have to be a lonely girl

There's a lot of good apples

On this old earth

I just picked a badun'

I wouldn't take you back

If you were Adam

I was gonna get rich and live in a mansion

Have more money than ole Jed Clampett

With that kinda dough I could get a movie star

Drive a red Lamborghini

Smoke forty-dollar Cuban cigars

You gotta get in line just to get in line

Just to find out you're too late

You gotta wait around till somebody dies

To get a good parking space

Don't you hate it when you've waited

In the drive thru lane

Just to find they forgot your fries

It's scratch and claw, dog eat dog

Backstabbin' big city life

Charlie sold Cadillacs for a livin'
The fast ones and ones made with style
But he wore out his own generator
And he couldn't roll back the miles
For Cadillac Charlie the sweet dream turned sour
Now he's washin' cars for six bucks an hour
It's hoop cheese and crackers and a bottle a day
And he sleeps in the back of an old Chevrolet

I've watched Casablanca twenty-three times
I know who's doin' what to who
Every day on Days of Our Lives
I cut the grass three times this week
It looked real good but then
I think I heard it growin' this mornin'
Guess I better go cut it again
I've got way too much time on my hands

There ain't no way I'll ever be
Rich as Rockefeller
But, honey that ain't no excuse
For treatin' me like Ole Yeller

Some folks are sinners
And some folks are saints
You are what you are
And you ain't what you ain't

I'll never get used to the internet
And forty-seven channels on my tv set
I'll never like the taste of that low fat food
And I'll never get used to life without you

Southern livin' ain't religion
But it's right there with it
Ain't no doubt
We were raised on dirt road faith
Where roots run deep in Holy ground
You'll never hear us talk it down
That's a sin here in the South

Acknowledgements

Many of the songs from which the excerpts in this book were taken, are songs I wrote by myself. The rest were co-written with one or two other songwriters, ranging from Country Music Hall of Fame members, Nashville Songwriters Hall of Fame members and dreamers, who had differing levels of success. I must give special thanks to Jerry Salley and Jon Randall, two of the greatest songwriters I know. The lyrics I wrote with them kept coming up time after time in my search for worthy material. A truly co-written song doesn't care who wrote which lines. Neither do I. My heartfelt thanks to those listed below. I tried diligently to list all my co-writers. If I missed even one name, I sincerely apologize.

– Jim

A

Brindley Addington
Trace Adkins
Jessi Alexander
Bill Anderson
Lewis Anderson

B

Max T. Barnes
Mark Alan Barnett
Phil Barnhart
Sally Barris
Kent Blazy
Bennie Boling
Roger Brown
Ed Bruce
Luke Bryan
Bruce Burch
Larry Butler
Jason Byrd

C

Carson Chamberlain
Kenny Chesney
Jameson Clark
Mark Collie
Jim Collins
Earl Thomas Conley
Tommy Conners
Don Cook
Gary Cotton
Charlie Craig

D

Linda Davis
Dan Demay
Nick DeWeese
Dean Dillon
Mason Douglas
Dusty Drake
Holly Dunn

E

Jeffrey East
Chris Eaton
Sara Evans

F

Coy Fuller

G

Dave Gibson
Rusty Golden
Lacy Green
Rodney Griffin

H

Gary Hannon
Stewart Harris
Chaplin Hartford
Wade Hayes
Denise Heard
Joe Henry
Sam Hogin
Monty Holmes
Wayland Holyfield
Harlan Howard

Mark Irwin
Sonya Isaacs

Alan Jackson
John Jarrard
Gina Jeffreys
Doug Johnson
Jamie Johnson
Brett Jones
Bucky Jones
Mark Steven Jones
Steven Dale Jones

Matt King

James LeBlanc
Brice Long

Peter McCann
Rod McCormack
Ken Mellons
Rusty Moody
Roger Murrah
Frank Myers

Mark Narmore
Wood Newton
Gary Nicholson

P

Andrew Pates
Bobby Pinson
Andrew Pope
Don Poythress
Curly Putman

R

John Ramey
Jon Randall
Kimmie Rhodes
Bill Rice
Jimmy Ritchey
Marty Roe
Deric Ruttan

S

Jerry Salley
Don Sampson
Leslie Satcher
Lisa Shafer
Blake Shelton
Joel Shewmake

V

Sharon Vaughn
Thomas Vaughn

T

Shane Teeters
Terre Thomas
Travis Tritt
Dan Truman
Josh Turner

W

Roger Alan Wade
Doc Walley
Joy Lynn White
Bill Whyte
John Wiggins
Walt Wilkins
Jack Williams
Kim Williams
Wally Wilson
Darryl Worley
Adam Wright

by Jim McBride

PUBLISHERS

Foster and Rice Music
April Music
ATV Music Publishing
Blackwood Music
CAL IV Music
CBS Songs
Chobe Music
EMI Music Publishing
Island Bound Music
Little Biscuit Music
Melmo Music
Mill Village Music
O'Shaughnessy Ave. Music
Rightfield Music
SONY
Spirit Music
Tree Publishing
Universal Music

PHOTO CREDITS

Payton Hoge
Jeanne McBride

Special Thanks:

Special thanks to God on High
for the gift of music in my life.

Thanks to all the great songwriters
whose work inspired me.

Thanks to all those who
helped me live my dream.

Thanks to Paul and Amber Brevard
at Joyful Soul Productions
for their great help in
preparing this book for print.

THE TENNESSEE HOTEL

You can stay overnight for a song
You can stay till you can't go back home
Oh, but only a few
Ever get rooms with a view
At the Tennessee Hotel

There's a lot to be said for desire
But the first time it's tried in the fire
Some give in to the doubt
They pack up and they check out
Of the Tennessee Hotel

Chorus:

The Tennessee Hotel
On the road between Heaven and Hell
They don't know who you are
Or they know you too well
At the Tennessee Hotel

There's a jukebox downstairs in the bar
To remind you why you came this far
But can you sing the words
In a way they've never heard
At the Tennessee Hotel

You can ask lady luck for a dance
But don't count on a long-term romance
Other dreamers like you
Wait to dance her 'round the room
At the Tennessee Hotel

Repeat Chorus:

Jim McBride
Cross Keys / Mill Village Music / ASCAP

www.ingramcontent.com/pod-product-compliance
Lightning Source LLC
Chambersburg PA
CBHW041334120726
48005CB00014B/2258